A Smile from Old Lowest

A celebration of bygone scenes, achievements and

By
Malcolm R. White
The Sea & Land Heritage Research Series
2005

GENERAL INFORMATION

Published by Malcolm R. White   Printed by Micropress Printers Ltd.
              Coastal Publications   27 Norwich Road
              71 Beeching Drive   Halesworth
              Lowestoft   Suffolk
              NR32 4TB   IP19 8BX
              First Published November 2005   ISBN 09547323 3 2
              Copyright © Malcolm R. White 2005   All rights reserved

Every effort has been made to ensure the information contained in this publication is accurate and for this reason numerous sources of information have been consulted. These include personal accounts of events, official documentation, local diaries, media resources and numerous accredited research works. However, when considering such a complex, varied and historical subject, 100% accuracy cannot be guaranteed. By popular request, all measurements, dimensions and distances in this heritage book are stated in British Imperial, not the European metric system. Books in this series are part of the National Published Archive and as such are included in the library collections of the British Library, the National Library of Scotland, the National Library of Wales, the Universities of Oxford and Cambridge, Trinity College, Dublin and, when appropriate, The National Museum of Science & Industry. Unlike the great majority of similar works, this book is not produced for commercial gain for the author or publisher, profits from the series are donated to charities and good causes.

OTHER TITLES IN THIS HERITAGE SERIES

DOWN THE HARBOUR 1955-1995   40 years of fishing vessels, owners, the harbour and shipyards at Lowestoft   ISBN 09532485 0X
A CENTURY OF FISHING   Fishing from Great Yarmouth and Lowestoft 1899-1999   ISBN 09532485 18
FISHING WITH DIVERSITY   A portrait of the Colne Group of Lowestoft   ISBN 09532485 26
CROWNIES OF LOWESTOFT   The steam trawler fleet of Consolidated Fisheries   ISBN 09532485 34
DRIFTING, TRAWLING & SHIPPING   A portrait of Small & Co. (Lowestoft) Ltd.   ISBN 09532485 42
GREETINGS FROM LOWESTOFT   A picture book of old postcards and photographs   ISBN 09532485 50
THE LOWESTOFT TRAIN   The railway at Lowestoft and scenes on the lines to Norwich, Ipswich and Yarmouth ISBN 09532485 69
LOWESTOFT ANTIQUITY   A picture book of once familiar scenes   ISBN 09532485 77
THE BOSTON PUTFORD STORY (1)   Fishing and Offshore Support from Great Yarmouth and Lowestoft   ISBN 09532485 85
LOWESTOFT CORPORATION TRANSPORT   Lowestoft Trams, Buses and Bygone Town Scenes   ISBN 09532485 93
RAILS TO THE COAST   East Anglian Seaside Stations, Sheds and Rail Links– Great Yarmouth and Lowestoft ISBN 09547323 08
THE YARMOUTH TRAIN   The railway at Gt. Yarmouth and scenes on the lines to Norwich, Ipswich, Melton   ISBN 09547323 24
                                        Constable and Lowestoft

PHOTOGRAPHS

Front Cover - The Royal Hotel, Esplanade and Children Corner in the early years of the 20th century. (MWC) **Title page** - Regrettably the great majority of this superb terrace incorporating a major centre of entertainment no longer exists. Many theatres and cinemas once existed in Lowestoft including the Palace, a substantial part of which was destroyed by fire in 1966. However, the impressive frontage facing the Royal Plain which is seen here in September 1969, was undamaged. The Palace opened in 1913, and after the fire and the demolition that followed, the majority of the site was used for a road and car park. (SJ) **Opposite Page** - A fine view across south Lowestoft on a hot and misty day in the 1890s with several people on the beach. Many of the buildings seen here have been demolished and one, the Royal Norfolk and Suffolk Yacht Club, was moved in 1903. (MWC)

CONTENTS

	PAGE
NAVAL LOWESTOFT	Inside Front Cover
GENERAL INFORMATION	2
ACKNOWLEDGEMENTS	4
INTRODUCTON	5
BYGONE SCENES AROUND LOWESTOFT	6
PHOTOGRAPHIC INDEX	Inside Back Cover

ACKNOWLEDGEMENTS

Much appreciated has been the cooperation and support offered during the preparation of this book by a number of kind people interested in researching and recording local history and Lowestoft's heritage. These include in particular, Mr. Peter Killby, the well known Lowestoft historian, and Mr. Stuart Jones BA, who has provided editorial support for the many titles in this popular series. Assisting or participating in this complex project have been Mr. Tom Drew, Mr. Stuart Edmonds, Mr. Norman Fairhead, Mr. Ivan Green, Mr. Peter Hansford, the late Mr. Ernest Harvey, Mr. Kenneth Carsey, Mrs. Hazel Thompson, Mrs. Muriel Twigg, Mr. Geoffrey Moore, Mr. Mark Osbourne, Mr. Peter Parker, Mr. Terry Reeve, Mr. David White, and the very helpful staff of the Lowestoft Record Office. A number of those helping are researchers from the highly respected Port of Lowestoft Research Society and the Society's comprehensive local research archive has been consulted.

PHOTOGRAPHIC OWNERSHIP AND COPYRIGHT

With the washing drying on linen lines at dwellings in the beach village, many sailing ships are seen in Lowestoft North Roads on a sunny day in the early 1850s. At that time many hundreds of vessels passed Lowestoft each day, and at times of bad weather the Inner Harbour was often full to capacity with commercial shipping seeking shelter. The town's major shipping and fishing interests provided substantial employment and brought financial stability. (MWC)

INTRODUCTION

In recent times we have been informed by press, radio and television reports that the previously rundown and in part derelict Lowestoft area is now "booming" with many major investment projects coming to the town and business activity at an all time high. A policy of cooperation with Great Yarmouth Borough Council on aspects of developing the local area has been set in place, with support already being given to Yarmouth on major projects such as the proposed port and international ferry terminal. Agencies have been set up to attract and support new businesses to the area and a major building to replace Lowestoft Town Hall is suggested and estimated to cost in total £40 million. The annual air show at Lowestoft is said to bring at least £9 million into the local economy for the two day event by attracting up to 350,000 people to Lowestoft. In addition to this, the many ongoing multi-million pound "regeneration" projects and major residential building developments in and around Lowestoft cannot fail to be noticed and are considered by some as being a truly great achievement. New roads are being built or are planned, and a retail centre and supermarket now occupy one of the town's historical sites. A local official and town leader has said that what is happening in 2005 is just a taste of things to come, with Lowestoft now considered one of the east coast's up and coming resorts set for a very prosperous future. The Council wanted the people to be proud of the town since it belonged to them.

A newcomer or casual visitor to the Lowestoft area upon hearing or reading these reports concerning the need to drastically change the town may be under the impression that in the past it was a dreadful place to live, work, or visit with a local population, industrial base and business community with no ambition, foresight or commercial sense. Long standing townsfolk will know different and remember with pride the many Lowestoft achievements, the town's spirit, special traditional charm and unique character, and the great attractions and major industries that made the town such a great place to be part of. This book recalls features and aspects of the Lowestoft area in bygone times showing that despite what is said today, the town has been lively, "booming" and prosperous before, and was much appreciated by those who lived there, and the hundreds of thousands of visitors that the town and surrounding area attracted.

Bygone "Sunrise" Lowestoft was not such a bad place!

Malcolm White
Lowestoft   November 2005

Bygone Days – Oulton Broad boating lake.   Bygone Days - Down on the beach, *The Princess Royal* public house.

This image taken from a glass plate negative in the author's archive shows a busy Inner Harbour at low tide around 1880. This area was later to be become the location of a world-class shipyard and one of the largest canneries in the country. Today these have been replaced on the right by the ASDA superstore and on the left by car showrooms and an office and business park. As with many other bygone major local industries, both the shipyard and the cannery provided long term employment for thousands of Lowestoft folk. Behind the various trading ships, sailing trawlers and the naval ship are Barber's Wharf, Sterry's Wharf and John Lee Barber's linseed oil mills destined to be destroyed in Lowestoft's most spectacular fire in May 1904. Denmark Road is in the background. *(MWC)*

At the north end of town, this picturesque setting shows the Warren House and golf course in 1907, well before Links Road was completed in the late 1920s. The building consisted of a number of dwellings and was located near a spring. Nothing obvious remains of it now , but for many years it was associated with the celebrated Lowestoft China. Today items produced at the Lowestoft factory, which was situated between Crown Street (formerly Bell Lane) and Factory Street, are much sought after by collectors, with quite small pieces fetching many thousands of pounds. The small factory was in operation from 1757 until 1802, although towards the end of that period work was concentrated on finishing existing stock. *(PKC)*

Royal Navy ships of the Fishery Protection Squadron have long been visitors to the town, in fact the Squadron at one time had a base in Lowestoft. However, *HMS Watchful* visited a different part of the town on 5th December 1889 when she grounded on the North Beach. Fortunately this attractive Fishery Protection vessel, built in 1883, was refloated. *(MWC)*

For many years in Lowestoft, one of the well known local businesses was that of Percy Wigg. Not only were they the main removal and storage contractors for the area, but also from their High Street showrooms they supplied fine furniture, and from their main office in St. Peters Street in addition to arranging removals, solid fuel could be ordered and delivered by their friendly coalmen. This comprehensive scene shows their fleet of removals vehicles in 1955 on Links Road at around the time the local council started to raise the level of the North Denes by dumping thousands of tons of domestic waste there. (MWC)

Whilst many residents and visitors may think that Gunton Cliff Esplanade has not altered over the years, there have in fact been several changes. These include the positioning of heavy guns there during the Second World War and in peacetime the removal of the much liked "Scotsman Gallery" viewing platform and shelter. A quiet day on Gunton Cliff is captured here in this fine view which shows the gallery and shelter. (*PKC*)

An interesting and busy scene from 1921 showing the North Beach bathing station, tennis courts and the salt water bathing pool. The area in the foreground occupied by allotments would within three years be used for the construction of the Denes Oval and incorporate new tennis courts. The location of the bathing pool, is now occupied by caravans. (*PKC*)

The expansion of Lowestoft's thriving holiday and tourist industry and the demand for better facilities continued and by 1934, when this scene was recorded, the Oval was in use for bowling tournaments. Teas, coffee and light refreshment were available from the fine pavilion. (*PKC*)

BOWLING TOURNAMENT ON DENES OVAL, LOWESTOFT.

SPASHETT'S SPECIAL PHOTOS.

Arnold House in the High Street was the home of the Arnold family, but today the building consists of a number of flats. The Arnold family had been connected with the town since Elizabethan times. Captain Thomas Arnold (1679-1737) is remembered through a sea fight against the Spanish in July 1718 when as a First Lieutenant of *HMS Superbe*, he led a boarding party on to the Spanish ship *Royal St. Philip* and seized the Admiral's flag as a prize. This scene, recorded in 1911, shows the house towering above the splendid gardens. (*PKC*)

The once wide open spaces of north Lowestoft are well illustrated here in this fine print. Belle Vue Park on the left, was originally laid out in 1874 on common land. The only buildings seen are the mill in St. Margaret's Road and just visible the roof of the mill cottage, St. Margaret's Church which was completed in 1483, and early houses in St. Margaret's Road and Yarmouth Road. On the left is the newly opened park and just visible on the extreme right, houses in North Parade some of which were built before the park was completed. *(PKC)*

Hardly recognisable as the Belle Vue Park we know today, this scene was recorded shortly after the park opened in 1874. (*PKC*)

The fountain was a feature of Bell Vue Park for many years but today is no longer there. Seen in the bottom left of the previous photograph, it was at the bottom of the steps and was later replaced by a drinking fountain. This is turn was later removed. This print shows the well iced up fountain still working during winter in the early years of the Park. (*PKC*)

84 LILY POND, SPARROW'S NEST, LOWESTOFT

The Town Council acquired the Sparrows Nest in 1897, the previous owner being a Miss Davey. It had been the summer residence of Mr. Robert Sparrow of Worlingham Hall and Baron Anderson together with his daughter also lived there. She later become the Marchioness of Salisbury whose husband was the Prime Minister. This view from the 1930s shows the lily pond with the much loved theatre and concert hall in the background. Many top stars performed in the theatre which had a special appeal as it was set in truly delightful surrounding. The theatre was demolished by the local council in 1991. (MWC)

61 NORTH BEACH, LOWESTOFT

Unlike today, in past times the north beach was an extremely popular venue for bathing. This scene recorded in the 1930s, shows just how popular the beach was. (MWC)

Christ Church opened in 1869 to serve those living in the beach area of the town, but these days not many families live in what is now essentially an industrial, retail and commercial estate. However, Christ Church continues to thrive by attracting a large congregation from other parts of the town. Planning applications submitted in 2005 indicate new residential housing in the beach area. This view shows the church set amongst dwellings and properties all of which would be demolished in the 1960s. (MWC)

At present, North Lowestoft Post Office in the High Street is the most easterly post office in the UK. This has not always been the case since the Lowestoft Beach Post Office, seen on the right of this print was further east. This Post Office was also a bakery run by Mr. Gissing. This interesting scene also shows, by the nearest lamppost, Emery's shop (later Squires), the Methodist Church and the almshouses, now the site of the Unilever factory. The person dressed in fancy dress with a bicycle covered with the union flag and red, white and blue decorations completes the picture. No doubt they have a good reason for such an attire and perhaps are participating in the town carnival.(PKC)

The beach community has been flooded on numerous occasions and this scene, recorded on 7th January 1905, indicates the problem well before global warming and higher sea levels became an everyday topic. The crowd appear to be talking to the person in the building who is perhaps unable to leave due to the water. A quantity of herring drift nets is hanging on the railings to the right. (*PKC*)

Most of the families in the beach community were associated with the sea for a living. Husbands, sons and fathers usually went fishing in trawlers, drifters or possibly worked longshore boats. These sheds are typical examples of the buildings used for the storage of fishing gear and were common in the roads and streets that made up what is usually called locally "the beach village". Just visible is a lorry belonging to A. & S. Boardley, a local haulage company who had a garage in the area. (*MWC*)

In East Street we find the herring curing premises of E. Butcher and on the left, the 1902 built North Beach Bethel. When this scene was recorded in the 1960s the clearance of the complete area of all dwellings and other properties was well in hand. As already mentioned, developers and the council already had plans to "regenerate" the area. (MWC)

The main building of the large curing works in Salter Street was always noticeable and fortunately this photograph exists today of that fine building. Soon after this image was recorded the building was destroyed as the area was cleared. A superb example of a typical flint built net store, is on the left, also awaiting the bulldozer. On the right is a wall constructed of brick and flint, common in many properties in the beach area. It has often been said that the town leaders made a substantial mistake when complete clearance of the area was authorised thereby removing much of the town's heritage. Today Great Yarmouth, Kings Lynn, and Cromer have attractive authentic heritage buildings related to their maritime past which are fully restored and open to the public. In some cases these feature gas lighting. (MWC)

This is the scene after the bulldozers and the demolition men had left having cleared one of the last parts of the beach village. Already new commercial buildings occupy areas cleared earlier of dwellings and cottages. Christ Church is no longer surrounded by parishioners homes and the remains of some beach cottages can be seen on the left. (*SJ*)

To the thousands of folk who travel along or live in the area around St. Margaret's Road, it may be difficult to believe that this muddy country lane is the same road. The only buildings seen are the mill and the miller's cottage and the church. (*PKC*)

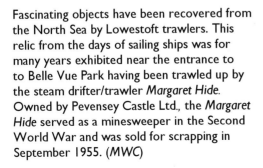

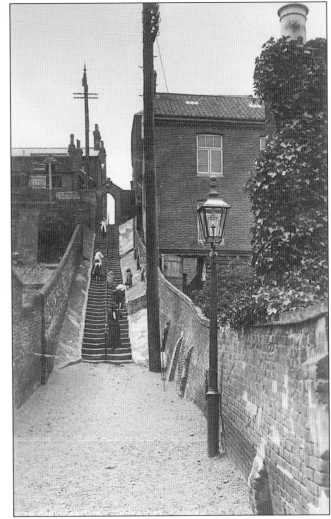

Fascinating objects have been recovered from the North Sea by Lowestoft trawlers. This relic from the days of sailing ships was for many years exhibited near the entrance to to Belle Vue Park having been trawled up by the steam drifter/trawler *Margaret Hide*. Owned by Pevensey Castle Ltd., the *Margaret Hide* served as a minesweeper in the Second World War and was sold for scrapping in September 1955. (*MWC*)

Lowestoft has footpaths and narrow roads running down the cliffs in the north of the town called "Scores".
One of these was in the news in November 2004 when the building next to it was destroyed by fire. Mariners Score is seen here in 1914 and the building is on the right The last use that the building had was as the Ashley Boys Club. When it was destroyed it had been empty for many years. (*MWC*)

Lowestoft Convalescent Home was originally a boys school opposite Belle Vue Park and the entrance to the Sparrows Nest. After the school moved to new premises, the building became a home in 1877 and was enlarged in 1882. The building still exists and was converted into flats in 1982. The extensive, well laid out grounds with lawns and wooded areas, are now occupied by High Street Surgery and Trinity Methodist Church. This morning view of the building dates from the early 1900s. (MWC)

One of the essential services provided in a well run town is the provision, security and upkeep of cemeteries. Lowestoft was provided with a new cemetery of 15 acres in 1885 with an additional 3 acres added in 1908. Further land has been added since then. This is Lowestoft Cemetery in the late 1890s, showing vacant land in the foreground that is now occupied by residential housing in Rotterdam Road and Hill Road. (PKC)

A detailed scene from 1949 of London Road North with evidence of war damaged buildings being repaired or rebuilt including Woolworth's and on the extreme right, the shops now occupied by Savers, Ottakers, Samuels and New Look. The much loved Odeon, demolished to make way for W. H. Smith and a shopping arcade, is having repair work undertaken by the well known local builder Leighton. At No. 85 London Road North, the fruiter and greengrocer J. G. Craik & Son Ltd., is seen continuing the long established Lowestoft tradition of displaying goods for sale in front of the shop, and an Austin lorry belonging to fruit and vegetable wholesaler Pordage is delivering fresh produce. On the right is the tower of the impressive Central Methodist Church, demolished in 1954 to make way for shops and offices. *(MWC)*

Vast numbers of "open all hours" corner shops have closed due to many factors including fierce competition from the supermarkets and younger people being unwilling to take over local retail businesses as owners reach retirement.

Seen here in July 1913 is the *Roman Hill Stores*. This was an off-licence and general stores in the Norwich Road area. A fine display of jars of sweets can be seen in addition to soda siphons and shoe polish. The posters advertising events at the Sparrows Nest include a concert by the "Society Idols" and a variety show entitled "Fairyland". (PKC)

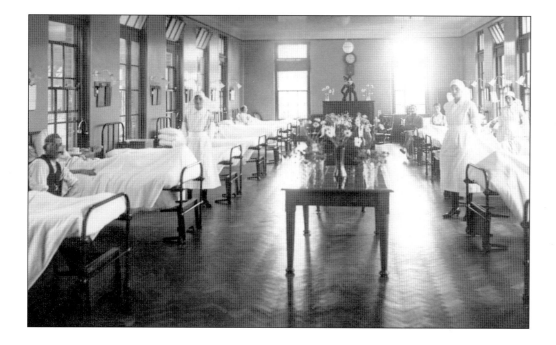

Completed in 1882 and opened by Princess Alexandra, the Lowestoft and North Suffolk Hospital has had a number of extensions over the years including those in 1926 and 1938. The first extension was a children's wing paid for by W. Youngman J.P. in commemoration of the Diamond Jubilee of Queen Victoria in 1897. Mr. Youngman was also responsible for other major gifts to the town. This superb view of a ward at the Hospital, complete with polished floor, shows how well kept and staffed they were in the early 1900s. (PKC)

A print showing an ordinary day in London Road North in the early 1950s with a number of familiar retail and other premises that are no longer to be seen. These include on the right the Young Men's Christian Association, George Armes Furniture store, Catlings department store, the Central Methodist Church and just visible on the extreme right, the Fleming, Reid & Co. wool shop. On the left we have an advertising board in front of Finlay's tobacconists shop, the Bus Station sign at the Eastern Counties parcel and enquiry office, and the opening leading to the bus departure and arrival area. Catlings was demolished in 1980 to make way for the Fine Fare (now Somerfield) supermarket, while the imposing Methodist Church, damaged during a World War II air raid, was knocked down in 1956. The Eastern Counties office was demolished in 1987 and the site was used for retail premises together with some of the land which was previously the opening. (MWC)

The Odeon was very much a flagship centre of entertainment and Lowestoft was fortunate in having such a luxurious venue which was capable of accommodating civic events and being used as a theatre and a cinema. Designed by Andrew Mather, it was by far the best cinema in town with a seating capacity of 1872 and incorporating many features of the Odeon in London's Leicester Square. The first manager was Mr. F. E. Barton, a man with a long theatrical experience who had appeared with Charlie Chaplin and Laurel and Hardy. Having survived World War II including narrowly being missed in an attack on the town centre by German bombers, the building was considered by those in authority not to be required and was demolished to make way for shops. **Left**-A happy occasion is witnessed here in 1949 with the opening of the Saturday morning cinema club for children. Both the Odeon and the ABC (Marina) cinemas had these clubs and both proved very popular with hundreds of children turning up each week. The author of this work attended the Saturday ABC club for many years during the 1950s and eventually became the ABC Senior Monitor, one of several older children given the job of keeping the other children in order! For this task a large pin-on badge was supplied and free admission granted to shows at the ABC. *(MWC)* **Bottom** - Inside the Odeon at Lowestoft. This fine building opened on 23rd January 1936 and was demolished in 1979. *(Studio 161)*

In the 1950s, it was usual for the circus to be accommodated on the field at the corner of Denmark Road and Rotterdam Road and sometimes animals were displayed in the town to advertise that the circus was in town. On one occasion two large elephants were taken for a walk to the town centre for display on the bomb site in London Road North on which Cooperative House (now Westgate) was later built. (*PKC*)

Also from the 1950s, this scene recalls the time when Arnold Street was a through road from Milton Road to St. Peter's Street The corner shop on the left is the grocery business of C. & B. Reeve, and their delivery van can be seen parked in Arnold Street. On the opposite corner is the business of Cleveland & Son, at one time well known in the town as general and second-hand dealers. The buildings seen here belonging to Campbell & Witham Ltd., remain today, but have been converted to flats. Part of the A12 trunk road now passes now through this point, with the terrace houses and shop on the right now demolished. (*PKC*)

A pleasant traffic free scene from outside the railway station in 1912. Of special interest on the left is the barrow boy from Lipton's grocery shop, the shop of the well known retailer O' Driscoll and the Dagmar Servants Registry Office. On the right is a branch of the London and Provincial Bank. At one time Tuttles furniture showrooms, it is now a pizza restaurant. The two fine Great Eastern Railway buildings in the left centre of the print and in front of the much celebrated Suffolk Hotel, were demolished in the 1920s. The demolition of the Suffolk began at the end of 1971 and the site is now occupied by MacDonald's fast food restaurant, having initially being used for Lipton's supermarket. In recent years much of the area seen here has been subjected to "regeneration", with the area being covered with concrete slabs and lighting installed to provide ground illumination. *(PKC)*

Flooding in the low lying parts of the town due to very heavy rain or tidal conditions in the North Sea has occurred many times. This scene of Tonning Street in the early 1900s shows one instance when prolonged heavy rain caused flooding in the area. In 1999, a similar scene could have been witnessed. Around the town new buildings have been built in areas which in the past, have been flooded. *(PKC)*

In order to build the present Boots store in London Road North, this fine Baptist Church was demolished in 1973. Built in 1899 on part of the Grove Estate, this building replaced an earlier one also in London Road North. A new church in Kirkley Park Road was built to replace the one seen here. (PKC)

In the past the port of Lowestoft was extremely busy and the berthing masters' job could be quite hectic. One of the best known was Captain Munnings, seen here at his office adjacent to the swing bridge in the 1930s. (ABPA)

The commercial pulse of a successful and economically strong town is a good banking network and Lowestoft was certainly well equipped in this respect. The name of Barclays Bank is well known locally, but many may be surprised to find that they had premises well placed in the appropriately named Commercial Road in the early 1950s. Trustingly, unattended cycles have been left outside whilst their owners pay a visit to the bank. Other aspects seen here of bygone Lowestoft are the spire of the Central Methodist Church, demolished in 1956, Walker Regis shop and the Lowestoft Corporation bus heading south down London Road North. A further interesting aspect is the once busy railway line in the foreground running between the harbour works and the fish market. (MWC)

The first bridge at Lowestoft opened in 1830 and as the town developed it was not many years before the narrowness of the structure started to cause problems. This glass plate print from around 1880 shows the bridge which gave access between the two halves of the town. In 1897, a new bridge replaced the one seen here. (ABPA)

A superb view of the first swing bridge in about 1870. The heavily wooded area in the centre of the photograph formed part of the Grove Estate and with development planned, removal of the trees started in about 1880. Missing on the left is Bridge Terrace, this had not been built at that time allowing the properties in Commercial Road to be seen. Behind the bridge cottages is the thatched Ice House, at one time this was used to store imported ice. (ABPA)

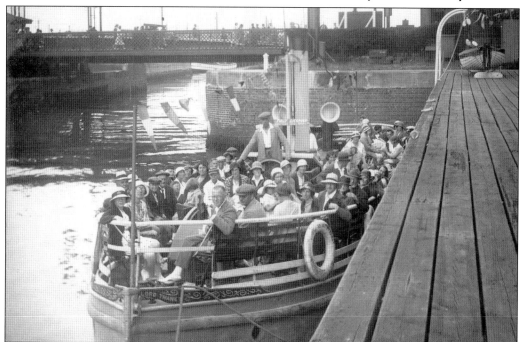

In the 1930s, Lowestoft had a thriving holiday industry and to cater for the holidaymaker the town could offer a vast range of attractions. These included sea trips, which left the South Pier every hour using motor, sailing or speedboats, and leisurely steamer trips from the bridge which travelled through Lake Lothing and the lock, on to Oulton Broad. The *Lord Thanet*, a famous Lowestoft steam driven craft, is seen during 1933 at the bridge about to leave with a full complement of folk on an afternoon cruise. *Lord Thanet* was built in 1902 at Birkenhead and was originally named *Ynys Mon*. She was broken up in 1953. *(PKC)*

A scene in the Inner Harbour about 1900 after a snow storm from the northeast had passed the town. Most of the sailing vessels are traders, but two trawlers can be seen on the right. Just visible through the rigging is *HMS Hearty*, built in Dundee in 1885, with work in progress on her topsides. On the left is the location where the *ASDA* superstore now is, previously the location of Richards shipyard, where world class ships were built. *(MWC)*

An Outer Harbour scene from about 1870 showing a barque, which appears to be for sale, and the South Pier together with the elegant Reading Room on the right. This building, an almost completed band stand and part of the pier were destroyed by fire on 29th June 1885. Prior to the fire the Reading Room had been a centre of entertainment for the gentry and upper classes, with well attended balls being held regularly there. The Reading Room was soon replaced by a new building. (MWC)

A fine print from 1913 showing the 1897 bridge closed to road traffic. Held up at the bridge is a United omnibus working the service 3 to Oulton Broad. The United Automobile Services took over the former bus service provided by the Great Eastern Railway to Southwold in 1912 and soon established other bus services in and around the town, well before Lowestoft Corporation had decided that the omnibus had many advantages over the tramcars they were operating at that time. (ABPA)

No book featuring past times at Lowestoft can ignore the great fishing industry. For decades this employed thousands of townsfolk and injected a vast amount of money into the local economy. Through the hundreds of vessels in the trawling and drifting fleets, the town benefited by building the ships in the local yards, providing crews, supplying every item needed to keep a ship at sea and also maintaining the large marine engineering industry to repair and refit the vessels. The fishing industry was indeed very good for the local economy. In books such as this it is usual to show trawlers or drifters landing their catches in one of the three docks or passing the pierheads. This print shows a different aspect with eleven Lowestoft built diesel powered drifters/trawlers in the Inner Harbour, all belonging to one of the port's major ship owners, Small & Co. (Lowestoft) Ltd. As with all of the past fishing vessel owners at Lowestoft, this company no longer exists and only one of the vessels seen here may exist and then in foreign waters. (*PTP*)

The area around Lowestoft has a great railway heritage, an important aspect of the district which is often ignored. With four stations in the area, three large railway engineering centres, an extensive dock network and the South Lowestoft branch giving rail access to canneries, shipyards, wood yards and two extensive goods yards, the many long gone major town industries were well served. A train headed by a North Eastern Railway designed Class J21 0-6-0 goods locomotive is seen here about to leave the Cooperative Wholesale Society factory and cross Waveney Drive with a large consignment of canned food products for distribution across the UK. The area seen here is now a Honda car showroom. (PCC)

The railway at Lowestoft had a very large workforce and in addition to footplate and station staff, many were employed in railway civil engineering. The railway sleeper depot on the northern shores of Lake Lothing covered a large area. Ships arrived at the depot with wood which was processed in the yard and left as finished sleepers ready for use in the rail network. With the use of a steam crane, sleepers are being added to one of large number of stacks around the yard. Later the sleepers would be treated with preservative. After closure of this depot, Shell UK built a major stores complex and a large modern office block by the lakeside, this in turn is now closed and at the time of writing the premises remain empty. (PCC)

Lowestoft Oil Mills

In May 1904 the oil mills belonging to John Lee Barber in Commercial Road were destroyed by fire. The building is seen here well alight with two of the Lowestoft tugs in attendance. The business was at one time owned by Webber, Hodge & Co. Ltd. Today the grain silo stands in the same location, which is opposite ASDA. (*MWC*)

BIRTE FLINT

These days the great majority of openings of the bascule bridge in Lowestoft are for yachts and other pleasure craft to pass through the channel. In the past however, a much greater volume of commercial shipping arrived or left the busy port with such cargoes as oil, coal, timber, fish, grain and scrap metal. In addition, hundreds of fishing vessels used Lowestoft harbour, ships of all sizes were built in the town and the port was once an important supply base for the offshore industries. All this activity made bridge openings very common and for locals it was all part of Lowestoft life. The German coaster *Birte Flint* passes through the swing bridge with a cargo of timber for Jewsons wood yard in the 1960s. (*MWC*)

An unusual view of the last swing bridge in the late 1960s. This bridge was replaced after failing and leaving the town divided. A temporary footbridge and a road bridge were put in place and the present bridge opened in 1972.
The premises of Ford Jenkins, Keys disposal shop, Thains restaurant and the coal office are seen in this unusual print. A well known and helpful feature of Old Lowestoft is the "Bridge will not open" board on the left. (*SJ*)

The Borough of Lowestoft town sign was situated near the swing bridge but was later moved to the grassed area opposite the BP filling station in the High Street. Featured on the sign are several aspects of the town's maritime heritage including fishing and the lighthouse. In the background is the temporary footbridge installed when the swing bridge failed. (*SJ*)

When the swing bridge failed the town was effectively cut in two and urgent action was needed to keep the town functioning. Before the Army could assemble the temporary footbridge, a temporary ferry was arranged using the *Norwich Belle*, a well known Great Yarmouth pleasure steamer. She arrived at Lowestoft via Oulton Broad, passing through the lock on 14th January 1969. Ferry passengers are seen here disembarking from the *Norwich Belle* at Town Quay on the north side of the harbour channel. The half-hourly ferry service started on Wednesday, 15th January, but did not run in the evenings or on Sundays and standing in the cold easterly wind encouraged many people to attempt the journey by Oulton Broad. (*ABPA*)

Locations that are passed by thousands of folk each day tend to be taken for granted. This view of the north approach to the swing bridge will be familiar to a great many people. Recorded in the late 1960s, the business premises are Yarmouth Stores and Thains fish restaurant, takeaway and coffee bar. The centre shop, here part of Thains, was in the 1950s occupied by the radio, television, and record dealer Reliance. The enquiry office of bus and coach operator Eastern Counties is on the left, and the spire of St. John Church is on the right. All the business premises were removed to allow the construction of the temporary and later, the new bridge. St. John's Church was demolished in 1978. (SJ)

Approaching the bridge from the south we see in the centre the remains of the roof of the Palace cinema which was destroyed by fire in July 1966. The large hoarding advertising Notleys, refers to the one time estate agents and auctioneers and not the present Notleys bar. The remains of the Palace cinema were demolished in 1971. Parade Road South remains in approximately the same position in 2005, the majority of the land enclosed here by the wall is now a car park and road, which Waveney District Council has plans to change. (SJ)

On the right of this print showing the Esplanade, is one of a pair of statues erected in 1850 on the completion of the first phase of the seafront development. The other is to be found on Royal Plain. Whilst these statues remain today, much else has changed including the style of the clothes worn today when compared with those worn by the Sunday afternoon strollers in this 1920s scene. (*MWC*)

Much has been said about global warming, rising sea levels and changing weather patterns, but in the past Lowestoft has endured floods and storms. This scene is at low tide on 29th November 1897, the day after a storm surge had flooded low lying parts of the town. Folk are watching the seas crash against the Esplanade and wondering what the next high tide will bring for the town. Other memorable dates for surges, storms and flooding include 1860, 1877, 1881, 1882, 1883, 1893, 1911, 1916, 1925, 1953 and 1999. (*MWC*)

A detailed aerial view of the "hub" of Lowestoft in 1969 with work starting on the retractable temporary road bridge after the failures of the swing bridge. A great many features of the town at that time can be seen including trawlers in the Trawl Dock, the prominent Suffolk Hotel, the burnt out Palace cinema, St. Johns Church and hall and the "Sizewell" crane. (*ABPA*)

A view from the early 1950s of the south beach and illustrating another of the varied attractions from bygone times that the Lowestoft area could offer visitors. For a number of years trips from the south beach out to sea were available in Second World War amphibious DUKWs, one of which, believed to be named *Speedy,* is seen here. Other resorts offering this unique attraction included Eastbourne and Hunstanton. Popular trips in DUKWs are still available in some locations including on the River Thames in London. *(PKC)*

Even before Jubilee Parade was constructed in the 1930s the beach and chalets were in great demand. The buildings up on Kirkley Cliff include from left to right St. Luke's Hospital, St. Mary's Convent for Girls, Hotel Victoria and the Kirkley Hotel. *(MWC)*

Thriving Lowestoft is well illustrated in this scene from 1934. When the first reading room was destroyed by fire in 1885, a replacement in the form of a new pavilion was built between 1888-91. This ornate building served the town well and was not demolished until 1956. Crowds are seen here being entertained by a band from St. Albans during one of the popular concerts which took place on the pier bandstand in the summer months. No live entertainment is provided today for the tourist on the Pier and no deck chairs are available on the beach or pier. (*PKC*)

An early morning scene from 1926 on the South Pier with only a few people about. This view is looking in the opposite direction to that above and shows a band perhaps rehearsing for the afternoon concert. The bulbs for the band stand illuminations are visible and the Yacht Club, built in 1903, can be seen in the centre left. In the past Lowestoft was well known for the comprehensive illuminations on the South Pier and seafront in the summer months. In those days there were not the numerous firework displays that have been seen in recent years. (*MWC*)

Bandstand and Yacht Club, South Pier, Lowestoft.

Lowestoft catered well for the holidaymaker and tourist during the 1950s in many diverse ways, some of which are illustrated in this fine overall view of the Royal Plain, South Pier and, on the right, Children's Corner. Coach tours were always a favourite and four different coach operators are represented here with their drivers inviting folk to participate in one of many attractive tours from Lowestoft. The coach operators are Eastern Counties, Norfolk Motor Services, Classic and Belle Coaches. At least two of the coaches were Lowestoft built at the famous Eastern Coach Works. Bingo is to be found adjacent to Children's Corner and the South Pier entertainment complex offers a vast variety of attractions including the "space tower". Just visible is another long established attraction, the human scales where your weight could be measured with British Imperial weights. For those who just wished to view activity in the busy harbour, one of the large fleet of trawlers is heading for the pier heads. This vessel is the *Lowestoft Lady*, a star of the BBC television programme "Saturday Night Out". As with many trawlers she was built in the town at Richards Ironworks, now the location of the ASDA superstore. (*MWC*)

A vast number of first class hotels once existed in Lowestoft and the Imperial was a typical example. The private lounge of the Hotel Imperial was considered the finest in the district and is seen here in 1925. This hotel was situated opposite the railway station in Denmark Road, but by the early 1970s the hotel and bars had closed and the building had been divided into retail units with fancy goods retailer Century 21, Rainbow Boutique and Kentucky Fried Chicken amongst the occupants. (PKC)

"The Lounge," Hotel Imperial, Lowestoft.   (Proprietors : Backs Ltd.)

Lowestoft has been fortunate in having excellent amateur dramatic societies. One of the fine performances in past times by the Lowestoft Operatic and Dramatic Society was at the Marina theatre in 1932, when "Rose Marie" was performed with Mary Cannell playing the lead role. In this rare print, Mary is on the stage surrounded by the supporting cast in their spectacular costumes. Many of the performances put on by the Society were at the Sparrows Nest, including "Good Night Vienna" during Easter 1938. In addition to performing in Lowestoft, Mary Cannell went on to make many guest singing appearances on the BBC and won the Miss East Coast and Miss Lowestoft beauty competitions. She later moved to South Africa. (MWC)

Today the Lowestoft Players have succeeded the Lowestoft Operatic and Dramatic Society and are well known for their professionalism and consistent outstanding quality in their performances. The sheer prolonged hard work put into their performances is to be admired. On a cold winter Sunday afternoon at the unheated Sparrows Nest Theatre, the dancers for the production of "Jack and the Beanstalk" are caught rehearsing their routines on stage. From left to right the dancers are:- Carole Cooper, Karen Ayers, Wendy Watts, Maureen Hart, Kathy White and Glynis Smith. The pantomime was produced by Maureen Miller and Avril Randall played Jack. Lactitia the cow was played by "Twiggy" Shrubb and Pam Hopper. There was a nine piece orchestra conducted by Paul Holman with the organ being played by Terry Hepworth. (MWC)

The dancers and chorus at a photo call on the stage of the Sparrows Nest Theatre. "Jack and the Beanstalk" ran from 30th December 1972 until 6th January 1973. (MWC)

As a major entertainment centre and tourist facility, the South Pier Pavilion opened in 1956 replacing an earlier building completed in 1891 and demolished in 1954. This view, looking north and recorded from the "Space Tower" at the Pavilion, shows the fine sea views, the docks and a Lowestoft trawler going to sea. The 1956 built South Pier Pavilion was demolished in 1989 and the lifeboat station, store and retail shop now occupy the site. (PKC)

During 2005 much attention was given to the high-tech water fountain system and the ground lighting providing coloured illumination installed at Royal Plain under the multi-million pound "Sunrise" regeneration scheme. In 1933, when this scene was recorded, the area had elegant iron railings and decorative shrubs to create a lasting genteel impression in several locations, including around the famous Royal Hotel. Some of these railings and shrubs were situated near the now closed underground toilets. The 1891 completed South Pier Pavilion and reading room, mentioned in the previous caption, is prominent in this view from the first floor Royal Hotel balcony. (MWC)

Major investment in Lowestoft is not new and well before the days of European, Heritage Lottery and other sources of grants and supportive funding, many major business concerns were seeking finance to carry out major works and improve the town.

The Claremont Pier was completed in May 1903 by the Coast Development Company, and here we see the building of the pier in progress. The seaward end of the pier, the "T" piece, was built at a lower level to allow steamers to stop there in the summer whilst travelling on the popular route between Gt. Yarmouth and London. (MWC)

For generations, Lowestoft's south beach has been popular with both local and visiting sun seekers and bathers. Whereas today the beach south of the Claremont Pier is accessible from Jubilee Parade, when this scene was recorded, little consideration had been given to building a wall or groynes to stop beach and cliff erosion. In the 1930s, construction of Jubilee Parade started with the wall eventually replacing the basic sea defences seen here. Claremont Pier was a major asset to the town and this view shows the full length including the steamer passenger landing section at the end, the Concert Hall, the shore end rifle range, amusements and the fine tea rooms. In addition to these attractions, many people came to the town for fishing from the pier. Other bygone facilities seen here are deck chairs, trips by beach boat and a large push ball and raft for swimmer's use. (MWC)

An attraction that thrilled thousands each year in the 1950s, the miniature steam railway was operated by Lowestoft Corporation and initially ran up the South Pier. Later the track was moved to the location seen here around the popular sea front putting green. A number of locomotives were used over the years but *Sonia,* seen here, was by far the most celebrated. A scale model of a London Midland Scottish Railway locomotive, after years of toil hauling trains of happy holidaymakers (and locals) at Lowestoft, *Sonia* was sold to a collector, exists today and is worth tens of thousands of pounds. One of the villas built by Sir Morton Peto housed the Lowestoft information office and is seen behind the train. This villa was one of a row, the others were demolished, as was this one later. The fine grass putting green, and the train have disappeared from the seafront together with the boating lake and well supported coffee shop. These have been replaced by the Royal Green grassed area and a car park. *(PTP)*

It was always an exciting time when a steamer arrived at the Claremont and this print shows such an occasion. The majority of the steamers were vessels of the "Belle" fleet although other owners operated ships on the busy route between Great Yarmouth and London. (*PKC*)

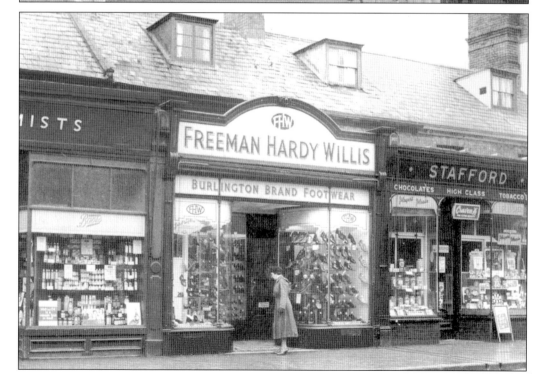

Kirkley has seen a great change in the shopping, banking and postal facilities available there since the Second World War. As a boy the author accompanied his mother to do the shopping there, and everything required was available in the wide range of shops, including Woolworths, several banks and the Post Office. Much money has already been spent in that area on improvement work and the local council has another multi-million pound project to further "regenerate" the area. Three shops in Kirkley, all now closed, are seen here in the 1950s. (*MWC*)

On Thursday 8th June 1922, Kensington Gardens was opened by the Mayor of Lowestoft, Alderman Selwyn Humphery. The site had previously been waste land but during the Great War was used for growing oats and potatoes. After purchasing the land, Lowestoft Corporation set up a scheme to improve the sea front facilities and using unemployed people started work on a project there which would create gardens, tennis courts, bowling greens, a miniature golf course, bandstand, pergola and rock pool. This scene shows guests arriving for the opening ceremony which was performed from the bandstand. (MWC)

Opening of Kensington Gardens, Lowestoft.

Not many years after completion, both the miniature golf course and bowling green are put to good use by visitors and townsfolk. Due to the careful forward planning by Lowestoft Corporation in the early 1920s, Kensington Gardens has remained an attractive asset in South Lowestoft. However, the popular aviaries on the north side of the gardens were closed in November 2001 and demolished. During 2005, Waveney District Council announced that they have plans to improve the gardens. (PKC)

PUTTING GREEN, KENSINGTON GARDENS, LOWESTOFT.

No book reviewing the Lowestoft area can fail to mention the serious loss of land and property at Pakefield due to cliff erosion. This was caused by the scouring of the cliff base, the soil above the scour being undermined and falling into the sea. Other causes of erosion were abnormal high tides. Serious erosion of the cliffs lasted for many years. Between 1824 and 1844 a loss of of 70 acres was recorded at Pakefield. The loss of land was only stopped completely in the 1940s when the sea wall built in the 1930s was extended south. This scene is typical of what happened at Pakefield for many years in the first half of the 20th century. Erosion is still happening at a number of locations in Suffolk and Norfolk. (PKC)

The traditional centre of Pakefield in the late 1930s and the one time terminus for the Corporation tram and bus services. Whilst the row of shops remains today, many other aspects of this location have changed. Gone are the telephone kiosk, police box, Corporation Guy FC bus, Terminus filling station on the right and Hughes garage in the bottom left. Instead of Betts fish restaurant, Blower's drapery, Ellis's fruit and vegetable shop and the Post Office we now have Mr. Chips, Pakefield Pharmacy and Pakefield Florist. The garage is now the location of Hildesley Court and dwellings now occupy the site of the filling station. Mr. Chips was at one time well known as Birds fried fish shop, and next door was Peaks radio, television and electrical shop, for many years specialising in Ferguson products. (PKC)

Posted at Corton Post Office on the 23rd January 1907 this fine postcard view of Corton Long Lane takes us back to the days when it was just a charming country wooded avenue instead of the increasingly busy road we know now. Unlike today, in 1907 the northern edge of Lowestoft's development was several miles away. *(MWC)*

The Warren House and the charming surroundings of the cliffs and denes have already been mentioned. The view shows this quaint building with smart fences around the three front gardens. *(MWC)*

Above - A superb sunset at Lowestoft together with the silhouette of the massive "Sizewell" crane on the South Quay. With road access from Belvedere Road, the crane was built for use in transhipping heavy plant and machinery used at the nuclear power station at Sizewell from ship to road transport. The crane was assembled in February 1962 and dismantled in September 1991. Lowestoft was the closest port to Sizewell able to take large ships. (*MWC*)

Top Left - Donkeys have traditionally been features of the British seaside resort and in past times Lowestoft was no exception in having these attractions. These scenes were recorded over 50 years ago at Wellington Gardens where donkeys gave rides in the summer months around the gardens. (*MWC*)

Bottom Left - In addition to other times during the year, model yacht races were held as part of the programmes for the very successful annual Lowestoft Fisherman's Week and the carnival week celebrations. Participants are gathered in the early 1950s for a race at the long gone Wellington Gardens model yacht pond. (*MWC*)

A classic scene of a sunset over a frozen Oulton Broad on a bitterly cold day in the mid 1950s. It is now many years since the Broad was frozen to this extent. However, in the past it was common especially in the harsh winters of the 19th century. At the Ice Carnival in 1891, a sheep was roasted on the frozen Broad and there were sleigh rides. A similar event took place in 1895 when a bullock and a sheep were roasted there.

Oulton Broad was incorporated within the Lowestoft Borough boundary in 1919. Nicholas Everitt Park was given to the Borough of Lowestoft on 10th January 1929 by Mr. Howard Hollingsworth to commemorate his friend Henry Reeve Everitt (known to everyone as Nicholas Everitt). The estate, which prior to his death in 1928 belonged to Mr. Everitt, comprised around 15 acres with a frontage to Oulton Broad of 590 yards and a road frontage of 290 yards. An entrance charge to the estate can only be made on twelve occasions each year. Howard Hollingsworth did much good work locally, including the gift of an operating theatre at the Lowestoft and North Suffolk Hospital. He became the first Freeman of the Borough on 9th November 1928 and died in Lowestoft on 4th June 1938. (MWC)

On the 3rd November 1914, men of the 25th Cyclist Battalion, the London Regiment, together with their mascot, march through Oulton Broad. At the time, the Regiment was staying at Oulton village and were about to move camp to Pakefield. *(PKC)*

At almost the same period and the same location, village folk come from their business premises to pose for the photographer. Little did they realise that over 90 years later they would feature in a book and be seen by thousands of readers. In the centre of the photograph are the Refreshment Room, to the right of that the Broad View Studio and Tea Rooms and on the far right, the premises of A. Allen, the well known Hairdresser and Tobacconist. On the left of the photograph is a sign indicating the boat house of Mr. John Gooch who lived at 4 Albion Cottages in the village. Mr. Gooch was the owner of a large hire fleet of yachts, sailing and rowing boats and an agent for trading and pleasure wherries. *(PKC)*

In the autumn of 2005, Waveney District Council revealed plans for a multi-million pound scheme to renovate, restore and enhance the gardens along the seafront and the esplanade. Two views of that area in the late 19th century are seen here.

Top - Looking south with the Royal Hotel on the left. Completed in 1849 and demolished in 1973 this building was designed by John Thomas and built by Lucas Brothers. The fine row of dwellings, described in 1889 as "a terrace of stately mansions with most tastefully arranged gardens - which are mainly in the occupation of families of high standing" have mostly been demolished.

Bottom – This view is looking north from where the car park opposite the Claremont Pier now is and shows a busy Esplanade. On the beach there are the bathing machines, bottled sea water is for sale at the hut and a concert party is advertised to perform on the stage adjacent to the esplanade.
(*Both MWC*)

Looking north along the sea front and the South Pier in the late 1960s with the miniature railway in the foreground and just visible in Children's Corner is the red and yellow striped Punch and Judy show. An admission ticket for the South Pier is shown below. (*MWC*)

In the opposite direction, the attractive seafront flowerbeds and lawns are a credit to the Lowestoft Corporation gardeners. The popular Esplanade Boating Lake, now part of the grassed area of Royal Green, is in the foreground. An admission ticket for the Boating Lake is shown below. (*MWC*)

The Post Office has always been a focal point in Oulton Broad, but on 15th January 2004 it moved from the familiar premises seen here to a new location in a local supermarket where it opened the following day. From the early 1900s when Bridge Road was unmade and the Post Office was also a telegraph office, a smartly dressed telegram delivery lad is seen standing to attention outside the premises. (PKC)

Looking north along Bridge Road in 1905 with St. Mark's Church on the right. Today usually a scene of continual traffic, when this view was recorded standing in the middle of the highway poised no real threat, as this group of five children are demonstrating. St. Mark's was completed in 1884 and was originally a chapel of ease to St. Peter's Church in Carlton Colville. (MWC)

Moving on to the early 1920s and at the somewhat basic Oulton Broad Yacht Station, a fine collection of sailing craft are to be seen including a trading wherry. Unlike today, much commercial activity in addition to leisure pursuits could be seen on the Broad, including the wherries, oil barges and Thames sailing barges. (*PKC*)

A fine view across Oulton Broad from the park in the early 1900s, with many yachts, rowing craft and a large Lowestoft sailing trawler present. In the centre is the newly completed Wherry Hotel and on the right the first Oulton Broad (initially Carlton Colville) railway bridge can be seen. A Thames sailing barge is on the extreme right at one of the important large commercial granaries on the Broad. (*MWC*)

A delightful bygone scene in Sparrows Nest and also an indication of changing times in modern Lowestoft. Due to various problems, these much admired ponds are now filled in, the waterfall and bridge have gone and grass planted where the lilies were and the goldfish once swam. (MWC)

Many folk will remember with affection this superb thatched shelter in Belle Vue Park. Today in modern Lowestoft all that remains of this attractive building are remnants of the back and side brick walls. (MWC)

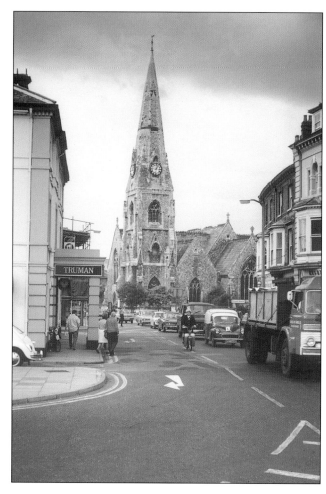

"Bridgers" have been part of Lowestoft life for generations and today the majority of vessels passing through the bridge channel are pleasure craft visiting the town and thereby boosting the local economy. Completed in 1854 and demolished in 1978, St. John's Church overlooks the usual traffic queue in 1974. This scene was recorded before traffic lights were installed at the junction with Belvedere Road and when the town saw, annually, many lorries making their way to the Birds Eye factory with peas. One such lorry is on the right. *(MWC)*

Lowestoft was home to major canneries and food processing plants. Employing hundreds of folk, these factories were good for the local economy and their products carried the name of Lowestoft throughout the country and abroad. The Cooperative Wholesale Society factory was a very large processing plant and part of the factory is seen here on a misty morning in the autumn of 1972. The factory closed in 1997 and was demolished in 2000. *(MWC)*

A major feature in the events calendar in the Lowestoft area has traditionally been the annual Oulton Broad Regatta and Fate. For a great many years the organisers have been very successful in featuring unusual acts and attractions and this scene from the 1950s is typical of these with a team of Royal Navy frogmen "performing" and diving into the Broad. Whilst the sight of these gents dressed up with flippers etc may have frightened some young children, their performances, which included recovering items from the bed of Oulton Broad, were greatly appreciated. Another major attraction on the Broad in the 1950s was the landing of a massive Royal Air Force Sunderland flying boat, and in front of tens of thousands of people the aircraft took off and performed a fly past and then headed off into the setting sun. This was a superb flying display from bygone Lowestoft and Oulton Broad, and a great experience for all. In later years, the Royal Air Force returned to Oulton Broad when the world famous Red Arrows performed over the Broad well before any thought was given to having a seafront air display at Lowestoft. (MWC)

KESSINGLAND BEACH   LOOKING SOUTH

A number of villages exist within a few miles of Lowestoft town centre.
Some of these are no longer separated from the town due to continuing urban sprawl. Kessingland has so far managed to remain separated with no housing estates filling the remaining land between there and Pakefield/Lowestoft.

The one time fishing village is seen here in the 1930s.
Top - A great many longshore fishing boats are seen drawn up on the beach.
Bottom - The charming tea rooms, beach area and fishing boat compound.
(*Both MWC*)

Together with the holiday/tourist industry, railway engineering and food processing, manufacturing and heavy engineering has been the mainstay of the local economy. As Lowestoft's once major industrial and manufacturing base has declined, scenes such as this are becoming increasing difficult to capture. A small part of the large full time workforce of Eastern Coach Works are seen gathered together in the body shop of this large bus and coach manufacturer. Work previously carried out at Lowestoft was moved away from the town and the plant closed in 1987. The site is now a shopping centre and retail park. (*NFC*)

Built in Lowestoft - The very last bus built with bodywork by Eastern Coach Works at Lowestoft stands in the work's yard prior to joining the fleet of London Transport. Over the years tens of thousands of buses and coaches were completed at the works. (*NFC*)

The local shipyards built a wide variety of ships for the world market. For various reasons, all the large yards are now closed. In addition to building tugs, cargo ships, fishing vessels, warships and other commercial shipping, luxury yachts and other pleasure craft have been built here. Today structures for the offshore energy fields are fabricated in the town and renewable energy modules have been assembled here. Great Yarmouth's projected new large harbour and dock area is likely to be the main base for this type of work in the future.

Built in Lowestoft – The world class 177ft. luxury yacht *Stefaren* was built at the the Brooke shipyard to a very high specification. She is seen here at the yard prior to handing over to her owners. (*NFC*)

Built in Lowestoft – The 259ft. long coaster *Pamela Everard* was launched at the Richards shipyard on 20th March 1984 and ran sea trials on 3rd June 1984. She is seen here early in the morning of her launch day in typical shipyard surroundings. Richards (Shipbuilders) Ltd. was a major shipyard and now lies under the ASDA superstore. This yard built a wide range of ships, both large and small, for the world market including a great many warships in war and peace time for the Royal Navy. It also built a substantial number of fishing vessels for the fleets of Lowestoft and Great Yarmouth. (*MWC*)

For hundreds of years visitors have come to the Lowestoft area and since the 1920s a major part of the accommodation offered has been the holiday camp. This view of the dining hall at Corton Holiday Camp in the 1930s shows a typical scene experienced in the many camps that once existed around Lowestoft. A number of very popular holiday centres, such as Pontins and Gunton Hall, are still attracting thousands of folk each year to the Lowestoft area. (MWC)

In wartime, the Lowestoft area was on the front line and a radar station was a feature of the local countryside and Britain's wartime defence. Although the station was referred to as RAF Hopton, it was mid-way between Corton and Hopton. The living quarters for the service personnel were in Hopton village close to the railway station from which many travelled. This view is from Corton, looking over Freeman's popular caravan site and showing the twin towers of RAF Hopton. Although the landmark towers have long gone, the station and all of the site is now in private hands with the station bungalow used as a dwelling. Much of the original perimeter fencing remains. (MWC)